Teeny Tiny Animals

By Lexi Ryals

Scholastic Inc.
New York   Toronto   London   Auckland
Sydney   Mexico City   New Delhi   Hong Kong

PHOTO CREDITS

Front cover: © Juniors Bildarchiv/Alamy, Tazzymoto/Shutterstock; back cover: © Barcroft/Fame; p. 1: © Juniors Bildarchiv/Alamy; p. 5: © Barcroft/Fame Pictures; p. 7: © Barcroft/Fame Pictures; p. 9: © Spencer Platt/Gettyimages; p. 11: © Richard Austin/Rex USA; p. 12: © A & J Visage/Alamy; p. 13: © A & J Visage/Alamy; p. 15: © Asia Images Group Pte Ltd/Alamy; p. 16: © M. Lammertink/Associated Press; p. 17: © DLILLC/Corbis; p. 19 © Angelika Krikava/Shutterstock; p. 21: © Mike Powles/ Gettyimages; p. 23: © Photolibrary/Oxford Scientific; p. 24: © Dr. Mariella Superina Ph.D/ Iucn/SCC Anteater, Slot & Armadillo specialist group/Argentina; p. 25: © Dr. Mariella Superina Ph.D/Iucn/SCC Anteater, Slot & Armadillo specialist group/ Argentina; p. 27: © Stephen Frink Collection/Alamy; p. 29: © Professor S. Blair Hedges/Dept. of Biology/Penn State University; p. 31: © Anthony Bannister/Photo Researchers; p. 32: © Juniors Bildarchiv/Alamy.

ISBN 978-0-545-24982-9

12 11 10 9   11 12 13 14 15/0

Printed in the U.S.A. 40
First printing, January 2011

Some animals are big and some animals are small. But there are a few special animals that are very teeny tiny. Some of them make good pets, but many live in the wild. Turn the page to learn about the tiniest animals from around the world!

World's Smallest Dog

Heaven Sent Brandy

A Chihuahua named Heaven Sent Brandy is the smallest dog in length in the entire world. She is only 6 inches from the tip of her nose to the end of her tail. She weighs only 2 pounds.

World's Smallest Cat

Mr. Peebles

Kittens are always small. But Mr. Peebles is smaller than most kittens, and he is full-grown! Mr. Peebles is one of the world's smallest cats. He weighs only 3 pounds.

World's Smallest Horse
Thumbelina

Thumbelina is so tiny that she was named the smallest horse in the world. Horses can weigh up to 1,000 pounds. Thumbelina weighs only 57 pounds. That means she is smaller than most golden retrievers.

Teacup Pig

Animal lovers in England can buy a very special animal—teacup pigs. These tiny pigs only grow to be about 12 inches high. That's about the size of a small dog. These piggies are also very smart!

Pygmy Mouse Lemur

Pygmy mouse lemurs live in the trees of Madagascar. Their long, skinny toes and fingers make it easy to grab branches. They are about 8 inches long including their thin tails.

12

Pygmy Marmoset Monkey

Pygmy marmoset monkeys are the smallest monkeys in the world. They live in the rain forest in South America. These monkeys are only about 6 inches long. They weigh about as much as a cupcake.

Monte Iberia Eleuth Frog

Monte Iberia Eleuth frogs are less than a half inch long. These little amphibians live in Cuba. They are so small that very few of them have ever been found!

16

Philippine Tarsier

Philippine tarsiers are best known for their large eyes. They are only about 5 ½ inches tall. But each of their eyes is over half an inch wide! This small animal weighs about as much as an orange. They live on the islands of the Philippines.

Brookesia Minima Chameleo

Brookesia minima chameleons live in the forests of Madagascar. They are among the world's smallest reptiles. Each chameleon is only about an inch long and usually gray or brown in color.

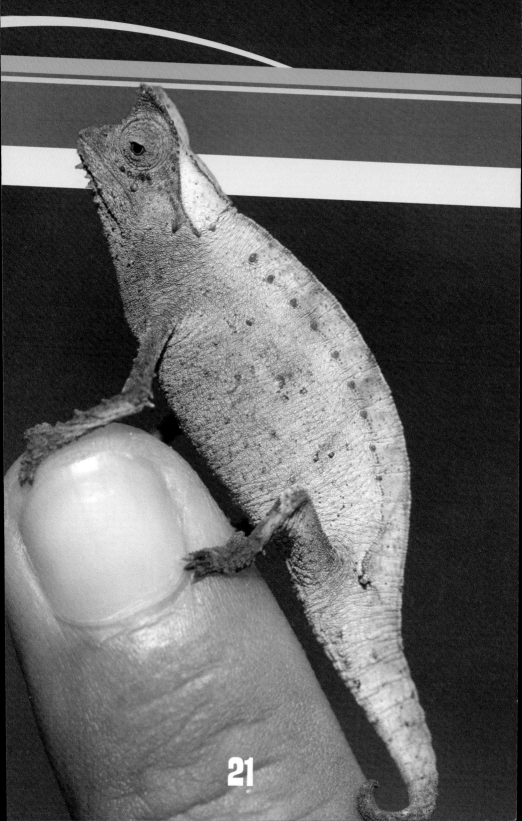

Bee Hummingbird

All hummingbirds are small, but the bee hummingbird is the smallest bird in the world. Bee hummingbirds live in Cuba. They are only about 2 inches long. Each bird weighs about as much as a large paper clip!

Pink Fairy Armadillo

Pink fairy armadillos are about 6 inches long. Each one weighs about as much as a pear. They have pink shells and white, fluffy fur on their sides.

Pygmy Sea Horse

These tiny sea horses are only a little over a half inch long. Pygmy sea horses live in tropical coral reefs. They are tough to spot because they look like the coral they live in!

27

Barbados Threadsnake

The Barbados threadsnake is the smallest snake in the world. Each tiny snake is about 4 inches long. They are as thick as a spaghetti noodle! These little reptiles live on the island of Barbados.

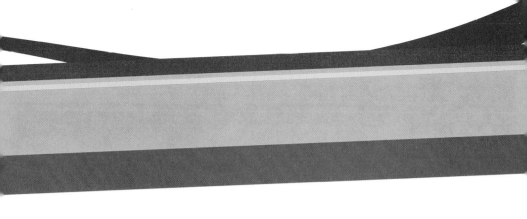

29

Speckled Padloper

While some tortoises are very large, the speckled padloper tortoise is only about 4 inches long! That makes them among the tiniest tortoises in the entire world! They live in Africa and are easily mistaken for little rocks.

Pygmy Rabbit

Pygmy rabbits are the smallest rabbits in North America. These tiny rabbits weigh less than a pound each. They are about 10 inches long. Pygmy rabbits have big ears, which help them listen for predators.